CONTENTS

Introduction 4

Comics 6

CHAPTER 1
Scripts: Not Just
for Movies 9

CHAPTER 2
Pencil Yourself In 19

CHAPTER 3
Ink It Up 27

CHAPTER 4
In Living Color 34

Animation 42

CHAPTER 5
A Creative Mind 44

CHAPTER 6
Raising Your Voice 50

CHAPTER 7
Getting Animated 58

CHAPTER 8
Setting the Stage 66

CHAPTER 9
Directions, Please 71

CHAPTER 10
The Wide World of
Production 79

Manga 86

CHAPTER 11
Writing Letters 89

Glossary 95
For More Information 97
For Further Reading 99
Index 100
About the Author 104

INTRODUCTION

Comics, animation, and manga are three entertainment industries that have a lot in common. They all involve drawn (or computer-generated) figures moving around similarly drawn worlds. Each medium also commonly features distinctive color palettes, visual styles, and unique stories. However, there are also major differences between these three fields. Comic books have deep roots in the United States, while manga is almost exclusively created in Japan—though both have worldwide audiences and incredible popularity. Animation, of course, involves moving pictures and is found on TV and movie screens.

If you've picked up this book, you probably knew all that already. However, if you're a fan of these entertainment genres, you may be surprised to learn that it's possible to forge a successful career in these industries without a college degree. Whether you're interested in writing a TV show, inking a comic book, or directing an animated film, there are positions available to you even without an advanced education. Instead, it's more important that you have creativity, an eye for detail, and an undeniable passion for the genre.

Though comics, animation, and manga are most easily defined by their visuals and designs, you don't have to be an artist to make money in these industries. Comics need scriptwriters, who cook up interesting ideas, map out the plot, describe the action, and compose dialogue between characters. The animation business needs show and film creators to come up with fresh ideas, directors to supervise the development and production of series and features, and producers to tie everything together. Manga, meanwhile, would never have found popularity outside of Japan without talented letterers filling in the medium's iconic speech bubbles.

However, if you do have artistic talents, you'll find yourself right at home in any of these fields. Comics rely on pencillers to sketch out action, inkers to fill in bold lines, and colorists to make characters and settings pop off the page. Creating an animated TV show requires the work of dozens of artists, including voice-over actors, background painters, and—of course—animators themselves, who increasingly use digital tools to make figures move in a 2D or 3D space.

No matter your interest or talents, if you love reading the latest adventures of your favorite comic heroes, watching the incredible detailed movements of big-screen animated films, or catching up on the complex story of the latest striking manga, there's a place in these industries for you.

COMICS

Superhero movies like the *Avengers* series and *Spider-Man* have become some of the world's most popular—and most profitable—films. As you probably know, most of this multibillion-dollar industry has its roots in the paperback comic books of the 1930s. The "Big Two" comic publishers, DC and Marvel, have been around since the mid-20th century, and their characters have become legendary in the decades since. However, comics are more than just superheroes and villains plotting world domination. This genre also includes comics in the Sunday paper and richly illustrated graphic novels.

At their most basic level, comics are a collection of illustrated panels laid out on a page. They're meant to tell a story by combining pictures and words in a particular sequence. They're commonly rendered with black inked lines and sometimes colored for a more vivid, dramatic, or realistic effect. Comics have the ability to use dynamic and imaginative imagery to enhance a written story, creating a visual experience that rivals—and inspires—films in its sense of movement, excitement, mood, and action.

The history of comic books can be traced all the way back to political cartoons, late-19th century comic strips, and science fiction stories from the 1920s. They came into their own in the 1930s with the appearance of Superman and Batman. Over the years, DC, Marvel, and countless other comic publishers have created comic series and, most recently, some series have been turned into record-breaking movies. Today, an enormous industry has grown up around the merchandising of comic characters, including toys, video games, and action figures. Comics, the characters in them, and their creators have inspired others—maybe even you—to let their imaginations free as they follow the adventures of their favorite heroes.

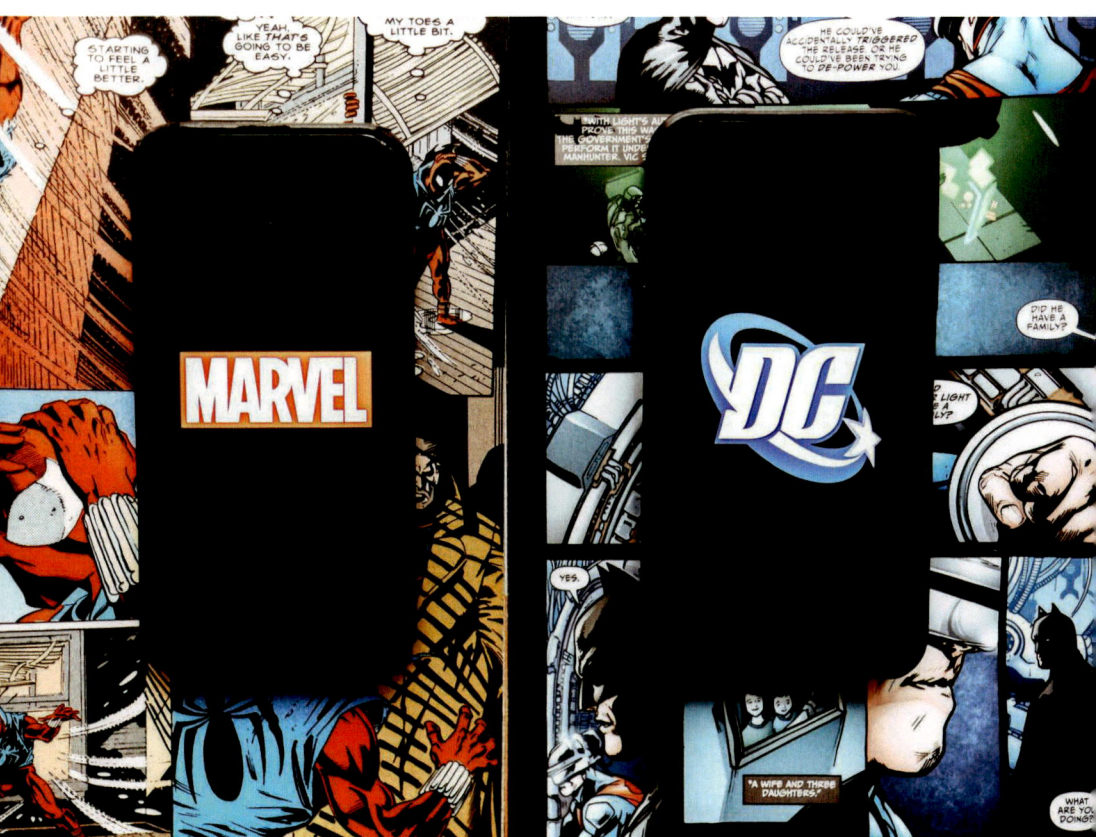

Marvel and DC are some of the oldest and most respected comics publishers.

THE YELLOW EARLY DAYS

Cartoonist Richard Felton Outcault created *The Yellow Kid*, a late-19th century comic strip. The comic's character—a street urchin who mocked New York City's upper classes—was named after the distinct yellow gown he wore. The character eventually achieved such widespread popularity that he increased the sales of newspapers carrying the strip. In addition to belonging to the first color comic strip, the Yellow Kid was also among the first comic characters to be profitably merchandised. *The Yellow Kid* appeared in newspapers between 1895 and 1898. Outcault is today considered one of the earliest successful comic writers, and *The Yellow Kid* is one of the oldest examples of the power of comics.

Because the industry has experienced so much success in the 21st century, comic production has become a wide-open field. Many artists are publishing their own work without major publishers. Digital distribution has allowed writers and storytellers to release their passion projects to the wide world. There are more tools and career avenues open to an aspiring comic author than ever before. Even though it can take a lot of practice and discipline to draw as well as the established artists, many great comic artists of the past and present never earned a college degree or trained at a formal art school. Instead, making it in this industry is based on your own creative vision, tireless persistence, and hard work.

CHAPTER 1

SCRIPTS: NOT JUST FOR MOVIES

One of the great things about comic books is that they combine pictures and words to create a finished story. Some comic books are written and illustrated by the same person, but many publications find teams of people to collaborate on a new adventure. If you find yourself more drawn to the written words of a comic—or maybe you're just not a great artist—then you may want to look into a job as a comic book scriptwriter. In this position, you'll be responsible for coming up with the plot, ironing out a narrative flow, and making sure dialogue between characters feels natural and enjoyable to read. On top of that, you'll describe what the artist for the comic should be drawing. Each panel and page should be explained in detail so that the words on the page and the images in the panels make sense.

WRITE IT UP

Making comic books is a long, multistep process. After your job as a scriptwriter is done, you'll hand off your finished script to the penciller. This person begins translating your written dialogue, directions, and ideas into visual form in a series of panels. Communicating your ideas is important, but there's more than one way of making sure the other members of the team are on the same page. Some writers prefer to hand off full scripts with specific directions, leaving very little to the penciller's imagination. Some scripts may even contain technical specifics like panel size and detailed captions explaining precise "camera shots" (descriptions of the way characters should fill a panel and what angle they should be seen from). Other writers prefer to write down only the basic plot and dialogue, giving the penciller a lot of creative freedom to expand the story visually as they see fit. There are also people who combine these two extremes, giving specific directions for some pages while leaving others open ended.

One of the most famous comic brands is Marvel Comics. Much of its success has been based on the creation of its ever-expanding Marvel Universe. Its "universe"—which includes TV shows and blockbuster movies—is a collection of characters who have common story reference points that unite them. Because they inhabit the same fantasy universe, characters often make guest appearances in other comics—without there being any conflict of

You can start practicing your scriptwriting skills from home. Start by coming up with big ideas and work on filling in the gaps later. Your first few stories will likely be unpolished—but that's okay. All writers have to start somewhere.

tone or narrative style. Many characters can interact in different works, making each of their individual stories and character developments richer. Creating a shared world is something you may want to keep in mind when writing your own comics. However, you shouldn't feel forced to have many characters sharing the same universe. Writing cohesive stories is tough, especially if you're trying to figure out how

A GRAPHIC LEGEND

Neil Gaiman is one of the world's best-known and most respected graphic novelists. He's had a long and successful career, penning dozens of comics and graphic novels. Gaiman has worked for several publishers, including DC, for which he wrote *The Sandman*, a popular series that became one of DC's top sellers. *The Sandman* is often credited with increasing the cultural and literary respect given to the comic industry. Gaiman has worked as a journalist and has written songs, poems, television series, screenplays, and several novels, including 2001's *American Gods*. In 2013, Gaiman revisited his *Sandman* series with *The Sandman: Overture*, though his most recent work has been in adapting his older work for TV and streaming services.

multiple characters can all meet up in a way that makes sense.

DOING MORE

Some scriptwriters are also talented artists and prefer to draw (and sometimes even ink and color) their own scripts instead of giving them to a penciller, inker, and colorist. Among the most famous of these writer-artists is Frank Miller, who authored *Sin City* and *The Dark Knight Returns*, both well-known comics. Many artists publish their work through independent publishers, earning them the moniker "underground cartoonists." These artists generally

Neil Gaiman has been personally involved in many classic comics, graphic novels, and other entertainment.

reach a smaller audience, but many achieve lasting cult fame. Among the most famous of these artists are R. Crumb (*Zap Comix*), Jeff Smith (*Bone*), and Art Spiegelman (*Maus*).

The most famous comic writer of all is Stan Lee, who helped found and popularize Marvel Comics, raising comics from a niche interest to a pop culture phenomenon. At Marvel, he cocreated Spider-Man, the Fantastic Four, the Incredible Hulk, the X-Men, and Daredevil. While he was admittedly not an artist, Lee's contribution to comics is undeniable. His career is a testament to the fact that even if you don't have a talent for drawing, you can still find a place in the comic industry.

GETTING READY

One of the best things about writing—including for comic books—is that you don't need an English degree to become a writer. However, you do need to have a strong understanding of language and grammar. A good writer should also be familiar with a wide range of comics and artists, past and present. It'll help if you read a wide variety of comics, graphic novels, and books. A solid foundation in literature, drama, history, mythology, folklore, and film can provide you with further creative influence and inspiration.

Visit your local comic shop and ask about the classics in the various comic genres, from old newspaper strips to newer digital comic artists. Do some research online to find out about up-and-coming new artists and their work. Check out interviews with comic authors to learn about their techniques. Take writing classes and share your work with others. Their feedback may be negative, but it'll help you improve. It's also important to practice writing your own stories, both short stories and lengthier works, and decide which method suits you best. Network with other writers at workshops or online. Don't limit yourself to comics—read plays, film scripts, and novels. It's useful to thoroughly steep yourself in the craft of writing—not just comic writing. The best way to do that is to read often and widely.

If you're sending your work out to publishers, there are some procedures you should follow. Most comic books are 22 pages long, and most editors will prefer that you submit a complete script. Be sure to refer to a publisher's website for their specific submission guidelines. Some publishers don't accept unsolicited submissions. Another way to get the word out about your new scripts is to attend a comic book convention. These events, which occur in many cities across the country all year round, are great places to make contacts, circulate your work, get feedback, and perhaps even chat with existing authors and editors.

In addition to practicing your writing and storytelling skills, you should make sure you have a solid understanding of word processing software. In the modern age, authors and editors send digital documents instead of hard copies. You should be

Comic book conventions can be fun, and they're great networking opportunities for aspiring writers.

spending most of your work time sharpening your script—not fiddling around with software.

It's important to stay confident, even in the face of rejection. It will probably take a lot of time to get your script into an editor's hands, and you'll receive many rejection letters before you receive a publication offer.

SCRIPTS: NOT JUST FOR MOVIES

GETTING PAID

Comic book scriptwriting is an ideal career for writers of all kinds who want to express themselves visually. Whether you can draw your ideas or not, comic scriptwriting can allow you to see your ideas come to life more easily than in traditional prose or poetry. Since the rise and expansion of the Marvel films, comic books and comic-related careers have experienced growth. More and more people are interested in the paper origins of their favorite on-screen heroes. As more comic publishers appear—and more comics are sold—there will be an increasing demand for good writers. If you can prove that your work is exciting and profitable, you'll be able to find a place in this booming business.

Competition is tough in this industry, however, and even if you can land an offer from a publisher, you probably won't make much money as a beginner.

Some top writers pull in big advances and steady income from their publisher, but this isn't the norm. You'll typically have to work your way up the ladder slowly, getting paid by the page or by the word. This is especially true if you're an independent freelancer. It's also important to note that if you freelance, you'll likely have months where you aren't paid at all—so plan accordingly.

CHAPTER 2

PENCIL YOURSELF IN

The production of most comic books—from simple stories to universe-spanning epics—is rooted in teamwork. Even most independent writers and artists have editors and proofreaders for their work, and having multiple sets of eyes on a project is the best way to make sure the end result is polished and professional. One important member of this production team is the penciller. If you're artistic, but maybe not interested in writing stories yourself, you may find success as a comic book penciller. People in this position are given scripts and asked to bring an author's words, descriptions, and vision to life. Pencillers are the ones who draw the people, places, and things that make comics unique.

MAKING LINES

Before a comic reaches a penciller's desk, it's nothing but words, or maybe a few sketches. The penciller's main job is to translate a writer's ideas into the visual panels that will eventually make up the comic book. The penciller will design the layout of the pages and guide the reader's eye through the story. They do this by appropriately framing action, presenting the content at good angles and perspective, and creating a sense of fluid movement.

Your level of freedom as a penciller will vary from scriptwriter to scriptwriter. Depending on the amount of detail they put into the script, you may have the freedom to come up with new and creative ways to arrange the comic so you're enhancing the impact of the story. Comics, just like movies, novels, and poems, always try to convey a certain mood, meaning, and message to the reader. The scriptwriter describes what they want to communicate, and the penciller brings this information to life, down to the last detail. Comic book penciling is much more than simply sketching lines on the page. The penciller's work makes the story breathe and the characters move. Readers are drawn into comics not just for the great stories, but for the highly detailed worlds created by the artists.

As one of the first artists to touch a comic script, a penciller essentially uses

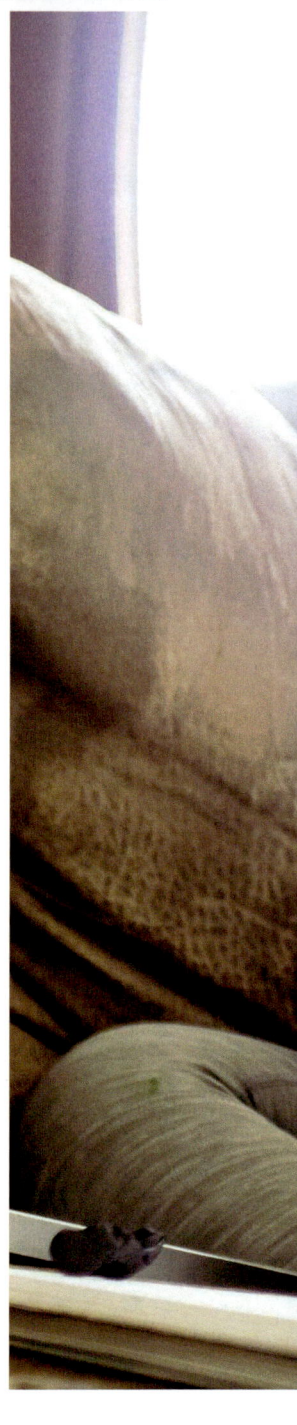

PENCIL YOURSELF IN

As a penciller, you're responsible for taking an author's words and bringing their vision to life.

SUPER PANELS

Believe it or not, the character of Superman has been around for more than 80 years. When he first appeared in the first issue of *Action Comics* in 1938, the comic book art form was still very young. Artist Joe Shuster decided to try something unique with *Superman*: he rearranged the layout of the panels on some pages in different ways. Instead of a comic book filled with a simple grid of identical squares on each page, a single panel might stretch the length of the page to show Superman leaping across tall buildings. Panels of varying sizes can now be seen across every comic. They're used to show depth and highlight dramatic moments.

Joe Shuster's work on the *Superman* series broke new ground for comic artists everywhere. Some of his techniques are now industry standards.

a sketchy style to tell the story. Some artists prefer to first plot out the story from the script onto scrap paper, working out how best to tell the story through visuals. A penciller will often use blue pencils on large sheets of paper to make their sketches. This blue doesn't show up on black-and-white photocopies. Later in the comic's production, inkers will go over the penciller's sketched lines in black, which does show up when the pages are processed.

As a penciller, you'll sketch out a rough draft by starting with ordinary paper and simple, rough squares as panels and make decisions on where you'd like each page of the comic to end. Should each page end with a mini cliffhanger? What characters need to appear on each page? How many panels should be on one page, and how will they be arranged? When you're ready to try a final version on higher-quality paper, use rulers to create your panels and try to clean up your lines as much as possible. This includes tightening up the lines on your panels (making them precise, clean, and detailed) and darkening lines around your characters. Cleaning your penciled work makes it easier for inkers later down the line.

GETTING READY

One of the most basic skills you should have as a penciller is the ability to cleanly and consistently render human movement and forms, including faces, hands, clothing, and architecture. You'll need to have a solid understanding of anatomy, perspective, and composition. When you're just starting out, it may be helpful to look into figure drawing classes, which can teach you how to draw the human form.

Before you're ready to break into the industry, you'll need to build a portfolio of your work. Your portfolio should demonstrate that you can handle a variety of character situations and styles, using your lines to tell a story clearly and dynamically. Work samples in hand, you can try to network and sell your skills at comic conventions. There are huge events, like San Diego's annual Comic-Con, and smaller local gatherings, so you should have a lot of options. Conventions aren't just for fans, they're also ideal places to meet other artists and potential editors.

If you want to submit some of your work to a publisher, be sure to check out their specific submission guidelines for freelance artists. Comic publishers will typically require final penciled pages. Some prefer hard copies, while others accept only digital uploads. Don't send inked, colored, or lettered pages if you're trying to show off your skills as a penciller. Remember that you want to highlight your strength as a penciller, not distract from it.

Be sure to have a professional attitude whenever you share your work. Portfolios should be "clean," with no extreme violence, gore, or suggestive content. You should also try to build your portfolio up with different styles and characters. A penciller who's able to draw men and women as well as animals and aliens will be more appealing to a comic book publisher.

Among the best-known and innovative pencillers in comic history are Joe Shuster (*Superman*) and Jack Kirby (*The Fantastic Four* and *The Incredible Hulk*). The work of these legendary artists is often available in book collections, which are a great resource to study if you want to learn line art and effective layout technique.

GETTING PAID

If you can find work as a penciller, you'll become an important part of the comic book production process. As the person who translates the scriptwriter's words and directions into pictures, your services will be invaluable. While some artists may use techniques that allow them to bypass pencils and head straight to ink, most comic pages begin with the foundation of pencil lines—and that's not likely to change.

The major comic book publishers Marvel and DC are seeing continued success with new issues of many of their classic titles, but they're always looking for new talent to help them remain competitive and introduce new stories, authors, and artists to audiences. Independent publishers—also known as indies—are also commonly hiring new talent to breathe fresh life into the medium.

Most pencillers work freelance, bouncing from comic to comic. Pencillers are typically paid per page they work on, and the pay rates are highly varied. Large publishers like Marvel typically offer between $160 and $260 per page—which can add up to a lot over the course of an entire comic. Jobs at these major publications can be hard to come by, however, because competition is so tough. There's greater opportunity at smaller publishers, but the pay is typically lower.

CHAPTER 3

INK IT UP

Once a comic has been imagined by a scriptwriter and brought to life by a penciller, it's the inker's time to shine. While the penciller draws out sketches and the basic layout of the characters, panels, and page arrangement, the inker's job is more subtle. They're responsible for going over the pencil on the page and making clean, bold lines in a dark black ink. If you're a detail-oriented artist with a steady hand, this job may be for you. As an inker, you'd be adding depth and balance to a comic book—and playing a major role in its overall production. Best of all, inking doesn't typically require any formal education. Instead, it's more important that you have passion and practice.

KEEPING CONSISTENCY

The process of making a comic book involves a lot of teamwork and interpretation. The scriptwriter has a vision, the penciller does their best to draw it, and the inker does their best to make the drawings pop. At each stage, there's room for misunderstanding or mistakes. Pencillers often leave notes on their pages, offering direction to the inker to help make sure the final outcome lines up with the original vision. Though they don't get as much creative freedom as their counterparts, inkers are vital to the process of producing high-quality finished work. Their detailed, strategic lines make comics lively and rich.

Inkers must be neat in their work, and they sometimes have to creatively interpret the work of the penciller. Importantly, there's a difference between inkers and tracers. Inkers have much more freedom to express their preferences in the artwork, especially in areas where they may feel the pencil work doesn't go far enough.

If you pursue a career as an inker, you'll need to know how to work with the different styles of line

The inker for a comic book plays an important role in its production. These artists help sharpen the work of the penciller.

work produced by different pencillers. As you follow the stylistic and artistic lead of the penciller, you'll also need to develop your own artistic techniques for adding light, shadow, and volume.

Though many comics are still inked by hand, the rise of advanced computer technology has led to an increase in digital workflows across the industry. The penciled pages are typically scanned into a computer at a high resolution, and inking is done using professional software, such as Adobe Photoshop. The original penciled pages aren't inked, and the electronically touched-up pages can then be sent to the next person in line (commonly the colorist).

Among the most famous inkers is R. Crumb, the influential underground comic artist who sprang

R. Crumb's ink work on many comics and graphic novels has cemented him as one of the modern masters of the art form.

out of countercultural movements in the 1960s. He draws most of his comics in ink first, bypassing penciling altogether and making him an exception to the general workflow that a comic goes through. Crumb uses a sketchy ink technique that enables him to work quickly. His distinct and expressive style has been influential and inspirational to many young artists. Another contemporary inker of note is Mike Mignola, whose *Hellboy* series (also made into a successful film series) makes dramatic use of high-contrast lights and darks, especially thick, heavy, black inking.

GETTING READY

Inkers must be skilled at line drawing and have an excellent awareness of shading techniques to give anything on the page depth and volume. Inkers should be able to work with a brush and, moving into the future of comic publication, a working knowledge of digital imaging programs will be essential. If you decide to become an inker, you'll be at the midpoint between pencillers and colorists in the comic production process. As such, you must be able to work collaboratively and effectively with other artists. Differences of creative vision and artistic style may arise, but an inker should bring a spirit of flexibility and compromise to every comic project they work on.

As far as tools go, you should try to work with what's most comfortable for you. Some inkers prefer pens, including brush pens, while others prefer brushes of varying thickness that can create different effects. You should be aware, however, that brush inking requires a lot of practice and learning. Beyond mastering inking tools, you'll also need to discover and develop your own styles and techniques, whether it's a heavy use of cross-hatching or experimentation with different line weights on the page. It will also be helpful to become familiar with inking sequential (multipaneled) pages, as well as stand-alone, single panel "pin-up" pages. Inking by hand can be slow and methodical work, but it can be extremely rewarding when you view the finished product.

If you're more interested in becoming a digital inker, Adobe Photoshop is a popular software program, and learning how to use high-end scanners will also be valuable. Any artwork that's transferred from page to screen must be kept at the highest resolution possible. You'll also need to work with the penciller to ensure the lines are clean and there are no smudges. The cleaner the pencil work is, the easier the process of digital inking. Look into taking a Photoshop course online or at a local community center. Try to become familiar with the finer points of using the software's many tools; the more experienced you are, the better you'll look to a potential employer.

GETTING PAID

Because inkers play an essential role in the process of making quality comics, they've often been in high demand. As long as comics are produced, there will be a need for inkers, whether of the pen-and-ink or digital style. Learning and practicing traditional hard-copy inking will be helpful to you as you start out, but keep in mind that technology isn't going anywhere. As production gets more advanced and streamlined across the comic book industry, you'll likely be required to work digitally. Learning as much as you can about basic art software early on will be useful in the long run.

As for pay, most inkers are freelancers and they're compensated based on the number of pages they work on. Because they aren't expected to do as much creative work, their typical pay is a bit less than a penciller's. However, because the line work they do is less time consuming than a penciller's work, inkers may be able to earn a similar amount by taking on more pages at a time. Rates can vary by publisher, but the better your work, the more you can ask for. Always be sure to verify your pay before you begin work. There's often room to negotiate with the publisher about fees and salaries, especially as your skills improve.

CHAPTER 4

IN LIVING COLOR

After the script has been written, the penciller has sketched out the basics, and the inker has cleaned up, textured, and shaded the pages, it's time for a person called the colorist to put on some finishing touches. Exactly as the name implies, colorists are responsible for adding color to comic panels to set the mood, highlight the action, and make the characters pop. Though people working these jobs rarely get as much attention as the scriptwriter or penciller, colorists love their jobs because they get to add flavor and a personal touch to comics while staying out of the spotlight themselves.

WITH FLYING COLORS

Ever since comics have become mainstream entertainment sources, their art and designs have become more and more sophisticated. That includes, of course, the field of coloring, which has kept pace with the industry by gradually becoming more of a computer-based job. Before advanced software took over, however, colorists would choose the colors they wanted to use in the comic's panels from a very limited selection of hues. Many colorists hand-painted their pages, used watercolors or airbrushing, or worked on photographed copies of the pages, making their color notes on the pictures. When photocopiers came along, colorists were able to work on paper copies of the pages, which helped them with the details. Colorists would write down color codes on the photocopies of the inked pages and then send them off to another person, who would do the actual color separation.

Color separation is the process that allows images to be printed in full color. Before printing, an image must be separated into the four basic ink colors: cyan, magenta, yellow, and black (abbreviated CMYK). Each of these single-color layers is printed separately, one on top of another. After the final layer of color is applied, the resulting page contains a full-color image that gives the illusion of a complete color spectrum. The color separator created the printing plates, which were commonly made of metal, plastic, rubber, or paper. These plates were used to transfer an image to paper. The results would be seen months later, after the comics hit store shelves.

In the mid-1980s, this labor-intensive and imperfect process changed forever as computer-based paint programs evolved. Starting around this time, computers could be used to perform all of the

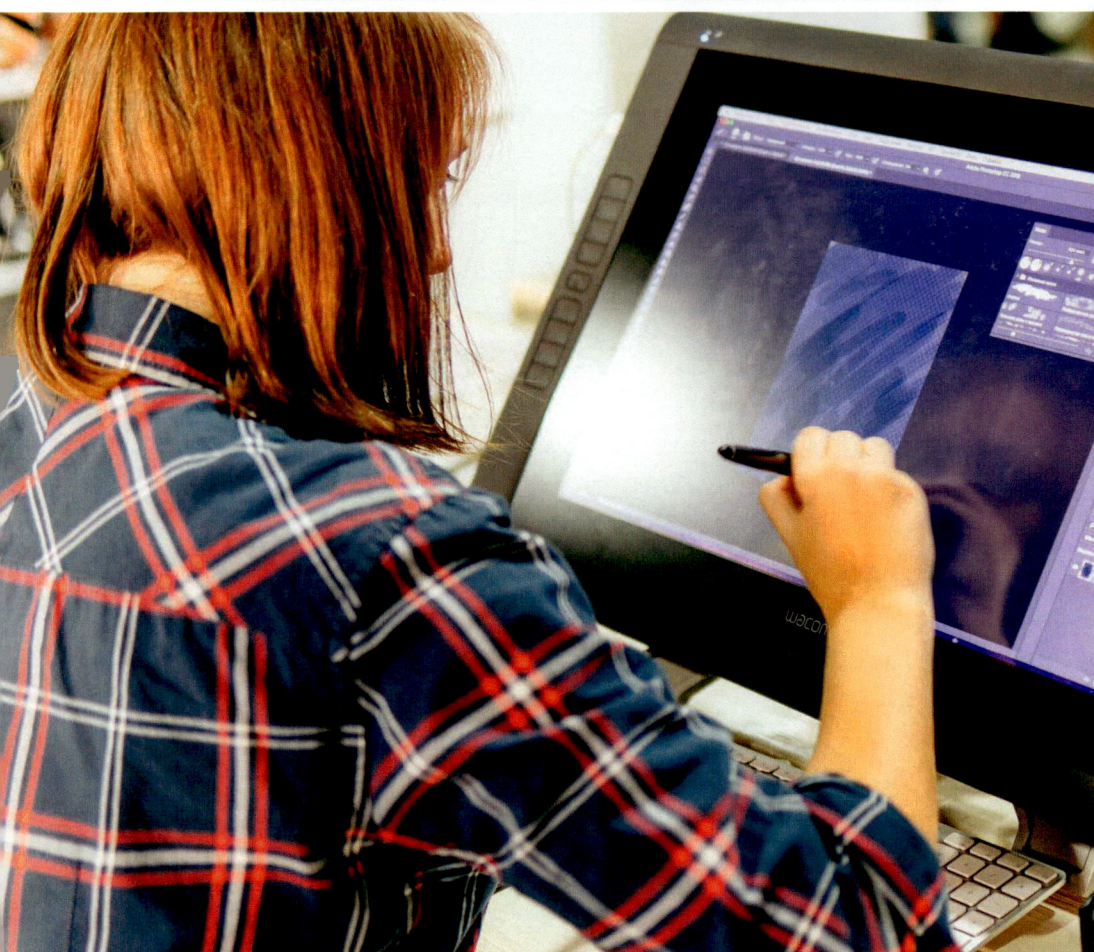

With advanced computer technology and digital workspaces, the life of a colorist has never been more convenient.

coloring work, including generating the printing plates. Modern-day colorists now use advanced computers and software programs like Photoshop to produce digital files called separations. These digital separations give the printer all the information they need to print the comic.

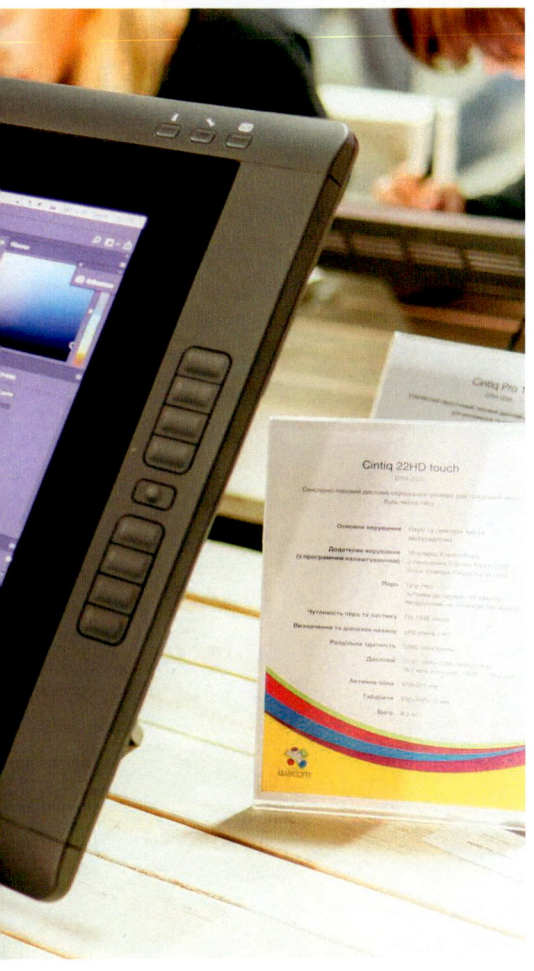

GETTING READY

Technology has made it easier to start up in many professions, coloring included. People with no formal training in painting can become colorists with nothing more than an artistic eye and a home computer. If you want to become a colorist, you'll probably need to invest in a quality computer and monitor, but it's no longer required that you own a wide selection of brushes, paints, and other traditional coloring tools. Having access to a computer will also allow you to use the internet to research design software, communicate with other artists, and share your work.

Photoshop is fairly standard for professional image editing needs, and it's popular among colorists. It offers tools to greatly simplify tasks that formerly required a lot of time and labor. There are online tutorials—both free and paid—for using Photoshop.

Advanced courses can teach you the step-by-step process you'll likely need to follow if you start working on comics. The general workflow includes creating color separations, beginning with preparing the finished line art and then introducing the colors, adding highlights and other effects along the way to produce interesting light and shading. You may be surprised at how quickly you can learn to re-create some of the effects you've seen in your favorite comics.

To be a great colorist, you should be able to identify and pick colors that will effectively help tell the comic's story and enhance and complement the line art. With the huge range of colors now available to colorists, you may feel intimidated to learn the ins and outs of how to color and what's available. Don't be discouraged; you'll likely find most of what you need directly in the design software you use. The most-used programs come with many tutorials and lots of easily accessible

Though most coloring work is done on the computer these days, you'll be better prepared to enter the workforce if you have traditional art skills.

information to get you started with using a wide range of colors. Of course, having a basic knowledge of drawing, painting, and color theory will help you decide how and where you'll use certain colors to change the mood, impact, or style of your artwork. It's also a good idea to learn how to use traditional illustrating tools—like pencils and ink—so that you can gain a complete understanding of all aspects of the comic production process.

If you're trying to submit some of your work to a publisher, try to find sample artwork online that you can use for coloring. However, make sure that you're allowed to freely use any art you find online. Most publishers will want to see how you handle coloring a variety of scenes, from action sequences to character-building moments. To impress a publisher, you need to convey a comic's various moods using color. Demonstrating a good mastery of lighting techniques will also help you make a strong and favorable impression.

GETTING PAID

As with many areas of comic book production, colorists will continue to be in high demand as publishers like Marvel push the popularity of the genre. If you want to make it as a colorist today, you'll need to bring digital skills to the table. With constant changes in technology, most of which make it easier to jump into the art form, it's a great time to become a colorist. If you take the opportunity to learn the latest computer coloring techniques and software, you'll be ready to learn new techniques quickly. Keeping up with the latest technological developments means staying even with—or even ahead of—the professional competition.

As with most comic book art jobs, positions in coloring are commonly compensated based on the number of pages completed. The pay you can expect to receive varies widely based on publisher, popularity of the comic, and other factors. Typically, the more color work a comic artist is expected to take, the higher your pay rate will be. However, you should keep in mind that coloring a greater number of simpler pages could pay you more than a smaller number of complex pages. You'll have to decide whether your digital coloring skills are better suited to fast work or intricate designs.

ANIMATION

Animation has changed a lot since its earliest pioneers started captivating audiences in the mid-1800s to early 1900s. In our current high-tech age, "animation" is a very broad term that covers a wide range of techniques and technologies. It can represent everything from Claymation stop-motion filmmaking (*The Nightmare Before Christmas* and *Coraline*) to traditional hand-drawn two-dimensional animation, often seen on TV (*SpongeBob SquarePants* and *Steven Universe*), to large-scale, big-budget, computer-animated productions (*Coco* and *Toy Story*). With the rise of powerful personal computers and the do-it-yourself independence they make possible, more and more people are getting into animation, both casually and professionally.

In addition to increasingly powerful hardware, computer technology is also benefiting from versatile and easy-to-use animation software. There are dozens of programs available—both free and paid—for people who want to get their animation career started from their own home. Technology is opening many creative doors and simplifying the animation processes, which used to be much more time-consuming.

However, even with all of the improvements brought about by technological advancement, there are still basic roles in animation that haven't

ANIMATION 43

Stop-motion animation is one of the industry's most visually unique forms. Making an animated feature in this style requires a very special set of skills.

changed since the very early days of the art form. These positions range from show creator to voice-over artist, and they're crucial to creating, producing, and sharing a finished film or TV show. As long as viewers are attracted to animated entertainment, these important roles will continue to employ thousands of passionate creators.

CHAPTER 5

A CREATIVE MIND

Nothing makes it onto TV or into a movie theater without being cooked up in someone's imagination. All-time classic characters like Mickey Mouse and Buzz Lightyear were born in someone's creative mind. It was only after months and years of hard work that they broke onto the screen and created millions of fans. If you're a creative person with a constant stream of ideas for stories, characters, and situations, becoming an animated show creator may be the perfect career path for you. You'll have to put in a lot of hard work—and get at least a little bit lucky—but the end result of seeing your imagination brought to life on screen will be well worth it.

YOUR GREAT IDEAS

The person who creates an animated show or film is just that: a creator. You'll have to develop the basic concept for the show, including where it's set, who the characters are, and what kind of situations the characters will find themselves in. This core information makes up the bones of your show. When creators are trying to get studios interested in their product, they often collect all this basic information in a document known as the show bible or series bible. All of this information needs to be thoroughly thought through and developed before it ever leaves the writer's room. Everyone who works on a production—whether it's a cast and crew of hundreds or just you and a small team—will use the show bible to make sure they're all on the same page. Information in the show bible should include names and detailed descriptions for the show's most important characters, including their personality traits, their appearance and attitude, where they live or work, and outline possibilities for plot development. You're essentially creating an entire animated world, and it needs to be populated with sights and sounds that will attract potential viewers. Don't underestimate the value of good characters in your work.

Once you have a show idea written down and you've made a series bible, your first goal will be to work toward a show pitch. This is a meeting with production companies that may be interested in developing your idea into a series or film. Production managers see countless pitches every year, so your goal should be to convey the essence of your idea to them as quickly and efficiently as you can. Some creators will have an entire script prepared for the first episode, called a pilot. Others will just have some characters and a setting in mind. Chances are, the more fleshed out, developed, and detailed your materials are, the better your chances of being offered a production deal.

You'll want to make producers as excited for what you've dreamed up as you are. If you've written a complete script, be sure to provide details on story structure, dialogue, and characterization. If you want to convey your idea visually rather than in script form, you might choose to present a storyboard,

If your show has a distinct visual style, you may find it useful to mock up a storyboard to show to potential producers.

which uses square panels on paper (comic book style) to illustrate the flow of the story. You might choose to create your own storyboard or work with a storyboard artist to create one.

GETTING READY

Show creators come from all backgrounds. Some are writers by trade, others are former workers in completely unrelated industries. One thing all animated show creators have in common, however, is a great idea that they're willing to work hard to get produced. You'll want to be familiar with a lot of different animated shows and films that you can use as points of reference for story and character development. Everything from classic *Looney Tunes* to *SpongeBob Squarepants* to *The Incredibles* will educate you in what makes certain characters succeed, what kind of voice talent helps bring characters to life, and what kind of creative decisions you'll need to make. As you start writing down your show ideas, it'll probably be helpful to also watch animated shows that you don't like. While this may seem counterproductive, watching "bad" shows will help you learn what won't work for your idea and what themes, character types, and writing you'll want to avoid. Production companies will be impressed if a potential creator knows what they don't want to do in addition to what they want to accomplish.

Keep in mind that you're the center of the entire production. Your team will be looking to you for guidance when it comes time to develop the show or film. If you want to succeed in this role, you'll need to be able to manage a team effectively while remaining open to suggestions from your staff.

Even though you won't be doing any of the actual animation, having an understanding of animation techniques—and what is visually possible—will be useful as you develop your show. You should participate in some online or in-person animation courses so you can learn the basics of the art. There are even free online video tutorials for an aspiring show creator, so search around until you find something you like.

When it comes time to actually write the scripts for your animation, there are a few options. Some show creators rely on others to take their ideas and build off them. Others prefer to write the shows themselves, or at least be part of the writing team. If you want to come up with your own scripts, you'll need to have strong writing skills, a working knowledge of word processing software, and familiarity with the standard format of animation scripts. Check out collections of scripts for existing animated films and television shows. Many of these scripts are available online. Overall, keep in mind that details are very important in scriptwriting. You'll have to make notes that detail the way a certain character speaks, their physical features, the clothes they wear, and the painted backgrounds they inhabit and move through. You may want to look for a job producing a series that already exists. This will give you an insider's look at an animation studio and how it operates. Then, when you're ready to flesh out your own show idea, you'll know what to write.

GETTING PAID

Animated entertainment has always been popular. With the rise of streaming services like Netflix, Hulu, and others, there's a greater demand than ever for good original shows. For producers and networks, the importance of a strong central idea, an effective creative leader, and a supportive staff cannot be overstated. The success or failure of a show largely hinges on its creator—and that could be you.

When an animated show is green-lit, or accepted and approved for production, it's standard to make a short run of episodes as a test. For a new show creator, salaries tend to be a flat rate. For example, you may be paid a set amount per episode, which will compensate you for creating, supervising, and maybe even writing the show. Once a show has proven that it can be successful, you can renegotiate your salary and be paid a higher amount and possibly receive royalties for as long as your show runs. Royalties are extra payments given to creators as their product (in this case, a TV show) continues to make money for a business (such as a production company or broadcaster).

CHAPTER 6

RAISING YOUR VOICE

When people think of their favorite animated character, the first thing that comes to mind is often their appearance and design. However, the actors and actresses who bring characters to life play an equally important role in the production of a TV show or film. Mickey Mouse's iconic "Oh Boy!' and Homer Simpson's famous "D'oh!" wouldn't be possible with the incredible voice-over work that's gone on behind the scenes. If you can give voice to unique tones, have a wide range of vocal styles, and love performing, becoming a voice-over artist for an animated feature could be the perfect career for you.

THE VOICE-OVER PROCESS

Though voices and sound effects are always perfectly synced by the time you see a cartoon on TV, voices for animated features are almost always recorded before the actual animation begins. In fact, the artists and animators who make the show work to synchronize their images with the existing voice tracks. The voice

If you're thinking of becoming a voice-over artist, you should get used to reading lines from a script in different voices.

track for a big-time TV series can be recorded by the entire cast at once. Some actors have the ability to play more than one role, but most have only one character to play in a particular show. The actors will work from a finished script—looking only at the words—and may occasionally be given a storyboard to study if a new character is being introduced or a complex scene is being set. The director or producer will typically run rehearsals with the actors and then supervise the recording session, ultimately choosing from among the many takes to get the final cut.

There are many qualities that a voice-over artist needs to possess, including the ability to interpret and portray a character's unique personality. This means studying the script, understanding the traits and backgrounds of the character, and making your voice reflect that information. It's also important to have creative versatility, meaning you're able to voice a wide range of characters, and an ability to take direction in the studio. Having an interesting or unique voice alone is often not enough to land you a role—it's your ability to bring a character to life that will make the difference for you.

GETTING READY

If you want to get interviews and auditions with the many casting agencies and companies looking for voice-over talent, you may want to research getting representation from a talent agency. You can't just pick an agency, pay a fee, and find success, however.

Most talent agencies will want to see that you have some form of training. This can be as simple as taking a role in your high school theater, participating in local acting classes, joining an amateur community theater, or auditioning for small parts in professional productions. This kind of background experience will demonstrate that you have some knowledge and practice with the art form. Once you've been accepted by an agent, their job is to connect you with clients looking for your particular voice-over style.

In general, you'll want to work on creating a short compilation, or demo, of the various voices you do. You can then send this demo to several voice talent agencies. Most agencies will expect a CD or link to an online collection of your work. If an agent likes what they hear, you're well on your way to finding voice-over work. When you send applications, include a simple cover letter that includes any pertinent information about your talents, such as vocal range, voice types, characters, singing ability, and the languages you speak.

You don't have to pay for expensive time in a professional studio to record your demo. Nowadays, you can make a demo right in your own home. There are plenty of inexpensive microphone options, and it's relatively easy to create high-quality sound files on your own computer using free software tools. You certainly don't need a degree in computer science or sound technology. Additionally, putting online versions of your recordings on a personal

"DUCKY": A SUCCESS STORY

Clarence "Ducky" Nash is one of many voice actors who achieved success in the field without a college education. Ducky is best known for his voice-overs of Donald Duck for Walt Disney Studios. After completing high school, he went directly into performing, though there weren't many animated roles for him to take yet. In 1933, he started working for Disney, and the rest is history. He gave Donald Duck a voice in 5 feature films and more than 150 short films.

His striking style, ability to interpret Donald's character, and range (he also voiced Huey, Dewey, and Louie Duck as well as various other animals for Disney) allowed him to reach the height of his profession.

Clarence "Ducky" Nash (right) is shown here next to his longtime collaborator, Walt Disney. Both men provided some of the most recognizable voice-over work in animation history.

website can be a quick and easy process. Having your own professional site makes it easy for agencies and other talent scouts to check out your material. Not all of this is free, but if you're serious about finding a job in animation voice-overs, it's worth the investment. Regardless of your actual on-the-job experience, you'll want your demo to consist of professional-sounding samples that best represent you and your vocal abilities.

If you think recording at home will be too tough, you can take a more traditional approach and pay for time in a recording studio—preferably one that's used by voice-over agencies. The people working in sound studios are experienced with voice talent and will offer the proper sound effects and background music to make your reel sound professional. However, this service comes at a price, so make sure you do your research to find a studio offering the best balance of professional treatment and affordable rates. No matter what, it's important to remember that your demo is both the potential entry point to your career as a voice actor and your calling card. Spending a little money on it is probably a good idea. Above all, it should hold your listeners' attention. If your demo is crackling and hard to hear, agents will spend less time focusing on your actual talent.

Once you decide you're serious about becoming a voice actor, you'll need to be available to go to many auditions, sometimes with very short notice. Auditions are held as frequently as two to three times a day if you live in major hubs like New York City or

Los Angeles. You'll either receive a script from your agent and perform the audition at your agent's office, or you'll go to a casting agency and be one of many other candidates. In situations like this, you're often given a script when you arrive and you'll be asked to do a quick reading in front of casting agents. These auditions are recorded. The voice casting agency will then send the audition demo directly to their client—typically a production studio—for review.

Whether you enlist a talent agent to represent you or you've chosen to find work on your own, the key is marketing yourself. There's a lot of competition in this field, so you need to make sure you're promoting yourself to stand out from the crowd. It can take a long time before you get your first paying job, so be persistent.

GETTING PAID

There are countless hopeful actors in the voice-over field, so competition for limited spots on TV and film productions is fierce. However, if you're determined and capable of working a flexible schedule, exploring your creative range, and transforming into various characters, then you're on the right track. Animation is a huge field, ranging from children's shows to mature feature-length films, and all the thousands of characters that make up these productions need voices. The wider your vocal range, the better your chance of getting job opportunities. There are always new animated characters taking their place in entertainment legend alongside beloved older figures, and there will continue to be a wide range of entry points into the field of voice-over artistry.

Voice-over artists are typically paid by the session. A session is the time period required for recording the character's part. Voice-over work for animation is regulated by the Screen Actors Guild-American Federation of Television and Radio Artists (SAG-AFTRA) and most productions follow the pay scales SAG-AFTRA has created. These session rates are often generous, but because work as a voice-over artist can be inconsistent, make sure you're careful about how you spend your pay after each session. Additionally, you'll probably want to join SAG-AFTRA, which is the industry's best-known labor union. Though you'll have to pay yearly dues and membership fees, you'll also be protected by the agreements and regulations the union has established with many production studios across the United States.

CHAPTER 7

GETTING ANIMATED

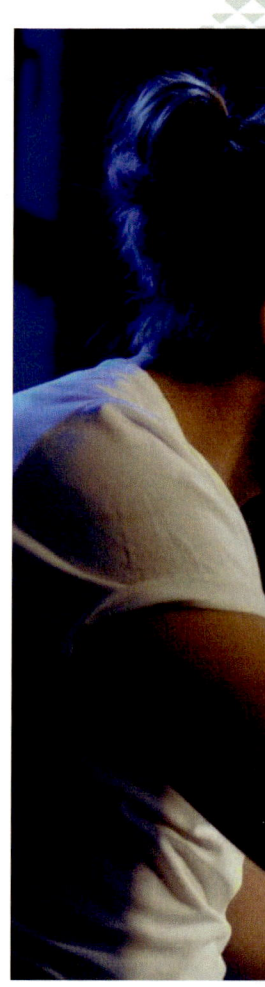

Have you ever thought about the way people and things move? Have you ever wondered how artists are able to make your favorite cartoon characters shift between poses and expressions so easily? If so, you may have the soul of an animator. These people work behind the scenes of TV shows and movies, taking figures and bringing them to life through motion.

DRAWN TO LIFE

If you're interested in becoming an animator, there are many kinds of animation to specialize in. Most people are familiar with two-dimensional, cel-based animation, such as that featured in *The Flintstones* and similar TV shows. A cel is essentially a single still shot of action that, when viewed in sequence with thousands of other cels, generates the illusion of moving figures and action. In short, cels make the animation happen. Two-dimensional animation typically uses "flat" materials, like paper or paintings, as the medium. The process of making this animation can be labor-intensive, and a lot of materials must be used to create the finished product. Advanced, versatile, and easy-to-use software has become an

A lot of modern animation is done on a computer, which has opened up the industry substantially.

increasingly popular tool for creating 2D animation, and modern-day animated TV series use digital animation techniques extensively.

Most 3D animation is also done on a computer, with Claymation being one significant and popular exception. Films like *Toy Story* and shows like *The Dragon Prince* feature detailed 3D animation that's generated on computers, and this has become an increasingly popular format in the last decade.

While computers have undoubtedly made it easier for many kinds of animators to begin producing their own work, you shouldn't neglect basic training in art, including solid drawing and composition skills. Along with this grounding in foundational artistic concepts, you should have a good sense of timing if you want to become an animator. No matter the materials or format, animators must effectively manage the number of frames per second (FPS) of their shows. FPS measures how many images can be shown and at what intervals. All of the action must be timed to fit the sound. Getting everything synced up requires careful planning ahead of time; dialogue and sound effects are measured to be correct down to the nanosecond. You'll need to demonstrate excellent attention to detail if you want to succeed in this field. More than anything else, however, an animator's most important quality is an intense passion for the medium.

GETTING READY

Some animators hold a degree in art or animation design, but it's not an absolute requirement. While the skills learned through formal education can be helpful when trying to break into the animation field, practicing on your own and getting hands-on experience can also help you land a job. Top-notch drawing skills will be among your greatest assets, so look into figure-drawing classes and seek out books or online programs that can teach you the fundamentals of drawing and character design. Pay particular attention to any educational materials that discuss how to make figures appear to be in motion, whether in stills or as part of animation. A good way to practice is to go to a public place and draw the people you see there, or head to a nearby zoo and draw the animals. Do a lot of drawing during your free time, whether you're watching TV, riding the bus, or waiting for class to start. In addition to preparing you for a career in animation, practicing your freehand skills is a great way to unwind and creatively reenergize after a long day.

Before you apply to any jobs, try to learn the ins and outs of cel animation. Learn about stop-motion and Claymation and how these formats work. Make some sample animated shorts on your personal computer. Show your work to friends and other animators—if you can find any—and be open to their suggestions. You may also want to look at creating

One of an animator's most important skills is portraying realistic forms, whether they're human, animal, or alien. Taking a figure-drawing class, like the one shown here, will allow you to practice your skills.

a personal website, on which you can share your work with the world.

If your home computer is powerful enough, you can purchase and use professional-grade software to develop your animating skills. You should have a thorough understanding of Photoshop, as

it's a great entry point for using more complex programs. It may also be possible to find animation and basic computer courses at a local community center. Animation festivals are also an excellent source of inspiration, and if you can make it to conventions like this, they're a great way to meet other animators and directors.

Once you've built your basic skills and you're ready to find paying work, you'll want to develop a demo reel to send around to potential employers. This will likely take the form of a DVD, but you may be able to upload a shortened version to a personal website. You should also be willing to network online or at conventions since you'll have to work your way up the ladder once you get a foot in the door. Be polite—but persistent—when shopping your work around to potential employers.

Generally, an employer wants to know what you're good at before they offer you a job. Get a feel for what your particular skill set is and sharpen it as much as you can. Don't try to be great at everything. Today's animation process is highly specialized, so focus on the specific aspect you're talented at, whether that's character design, 3D modeling, or shading. Keep it simple: if you love the art of animating, improve your ability to show the character's movements, and don't distract from your basic talent with a lot of showy effects that might get in the way of clean storytelling.

GETTING PAID

Good animators will always be in high demand, and the Bureau of Labor Statistics reports that the industry will see an overall 4 percent growth rate between 2018 and 2028. However, competition in the business can be steep, with many talented people trying to get into the field. Your biggest challenge will be standing out from the crowd, but the internet has made it easier to distribute your personal work. Many animators—even on some big-budget films—are freelance artists. As such, they may command higher rates, but freelancers often don't share the benefits (including strong job security) of in-house employees. On the other hand, being a freelancer enables you to work on a wider variety of projects than you might work on otherwise and to make more contacts throughout the industry, increasing your future opportunities.

Most animators, whether they're freelance or full-time employees, are paid based on the size of a production's budget and how many other freelancers are employed to work on the same feature. Generally, the compensation is substantial for workers in this industry. The average salary for a TV and film animator in 2018 was $77,860. However, since there's no guarantee that any given show or film will become a multiyear series, there may be times when you're in between jobs if you become a freelance animator.

CHAPTER 8

SETTING THE STAGE

Though animated characters get most of the attention on TV shows and in films, the scenes in which the action takes place are also highly important. Most animated productions feature dozens of scenes, ranging from simple home interiors to sweeping alien planets. A background artist is a specialized animation expert who works with other designers to come up with the backdrops that help define a series or movie. This may be the correct career for you if you're interested in drawing, painting, and digital art, but you're not especially interested in character design or animating figures.

MORE THAN A BACKDROP

Backgrounds in both TV shows and films are typically created in phases. Sometimes, one person is responsible for all the steps in the background work. Other times, it's split up among various artists. Either way, if you want to become a background artist, it's important that you're familiar with all of the different phases in the background creation process. Though you may only be responsible for one phase at a particular job, you'll likely be asked to work on each of them over the course of your career.

The first phase is the layout of the initial design for the background. Layouts are typically done as line drawings. These drawings are important because they set the mood and capture the appropriate perspective for the scene. Next comes inking; during this phase, the line drawings are cleaned up and heavier lines are added to the background. This process is followed by rough coloring, which gets reviewed by the director. Once the background has been approved, the final paint with shading is added by the background artist. This final step is critical to establishing the look and overall mood of the production.

Background artists sometimes use traditional paints and airbrushes to achieve their desired effects. There are 2D and 3D paint software programs available to professional background artists, and experience using a drawing tablet will be very useful in your early career.

GETTING READY

To become a background artist, you should first learn the basic principles of painting and color theory. Employers will also want you to have a good understanding of the layout process, which defines the

You should have a solid grasp of basic drawing and painting skills if you want to illustrate backgrounds. Try your hand at depicting landscapes like this.

initial requirements for making background scenes. Because most modern productions use at least some form of computer art and animation, you'll also need to be proficient with the many software programs professional artists use.

You may find it helpful to take basic art classes, such as perspective drawing. You'll want to learn

SETTING THE STAGE

how to draw all kinds of objects in all kinds of settings. Study lighting techniques used in animated and live-action films. While you may find work with a company willing to give you training, don't count on it. Through classes, hands-on experience, and hours of practice, you'll likely have to train yourself. The good news, however, is that this path will show that you're a self-starter, and it'll also help you create a portfolio that shows off your previous projects. Employers will be looking for both of these things during the hiring process.

GETTING PAID

Most artistic fields are highly competitive, and this is no exception. However, more and more animated productions are being made, and there will continue to be a need for specialized talent like background artists. The field of animation is becoming increasingly specialized, especially when it comes to complex productions like feature-length films. Productions like these can require a staff of hundreds, from multiple storyboard and background artists to artists who specialize in creating digital lighting effects.

Because there are so many different kinds of productions and artists, there's no standard compensation package for background artists. Some artists like to be paid per background, which means TV shows and movies with multiple scenes will be the most lucrative. Others prefer a more traditional weekly payment, which allows them to have a steady income for the length of a project. Still others want to be paid per episode for a predetermined number of backgrounds. Their project rate would be paid up front based on the number of backgrounds required. If more backgrounds are needed, they can be given an additional fee per background.

CHAPTER 9

DIRECTIONS, PLEASE

Most shows and films include a brief roll of credits near the start. Thousands of people can contribute to the production of an animated project, but the names listed at the beginning are the ones most integral to the success of any TV program or movie: the actors, creators, writers, and—maybe most importantly—the director. The person who serves in this role must be a manager, organizer, motivator, and more. They're in charge of creative direction and quality control. Every frame of animation must pass through the director, making this job one of the most demanding—but most prestigious—in the industry.

DIRECTOR DUTIES

Directors are responsible for planning and designing a production. They're often involved in a project from initial concept to final completion. They interpret the script or storyboard and try to preserve the original vision of the creators, writers, and artists.

Directors must be able to effectively lead their staff, which can include a wide variety of people. They encourage their artists, writers, and actors to work together.

They may become involved with all aspects of the project, including design, storyboards, layout, animation, and postproduction. They may also provide direction on music and sound effects.

If you want to become a director, you must have strong interpersonal, managerial, and organizational

skills. You'll be working closely with the producer to help manage key aspects of the project. This often includes keeping the schedule—and budget—for the project on track. You should feel comfortable speaking in front of a group, as part of your responsibilities will be to guide and direct free-ranging creative meetings with your staff.

Directors also need to be highly creative, have good storytelling ability, and have a solid understanding of how animations are made. While you don't have to personally master all of the technologies and techniques used in an animated production, you should have a working knowledge of the software, artistic techniques, and technical limitations that your staff will be using and facing. If an animator has a problem, for example, they may ask you how to solve it. If you're familiar with the process behind what they're trying to do, you'll be able to come up with a solution or a workaround. As a director, you should have a good sense of timing, as much of the animation process hinges on the split-second choreography between character movement, music, and sound effects. Each component of an animated film or TV show must work in harmony for maximum comic or dramatic effect.

What does an animation director do on a daily basis? Here's a list of core tasks they may be responsible for during the production of an animated work:

- Identify and recruit talent (including vocal talent)
- Consult on the preliminary storyboard
- Review character designs
- Review prop designs
- Oversee day-to-day activities of animators
- Review background art
- Guide everyone on staff to understand and follow the project's vision while taking into account their feedback on the production process

GETTING READY

Solid creative abilities and good project management skills make up the foundation of a good animation director's skill set. You likely won't be doing any animation yourself, but you need to have a reasonable idea of what you can expect of your animators.

THE LEGACY OF WALT DISNEY

Walt Disney was one of the earliest animation pioneers. As an artist, producer, and director, his films and TV series paved the way for future generations of animators. Countless artists have been inspired by his unique character design, simple execution, and sense of humor. His best-known creation—Mickey Mouse—first appeared in short cartoons in 1928, launching Disney to unprecedented success that continues to this day. On top of his credits as director, he was the original voice of Mickey Mouse, and he strengthened the reputation of cartoon creators throughout his long career.

This means having background knowledge about the capabilities of both your staff and the tools they're using. For example, you wouldn't want to ask an animator to put hundreds of characters on screen at once if their talent lies in highly detailed background art.

A thorough understanding of the entire animation process will be to your benefit. Whether it's a 2D or 3D production, Claymation, or anything in between, your knowledge of the art form will be the basis of the entire production. Being knowledgeable will inspire your staff and help you gain their confidence and trust.

Before you try to get into professional directing, you'll want to have a few smaller projects under your belt. Your potential employers will want to see demonstrations of your creative talent and your practical project management abilities. Create a portfolio with a sampling of your work before you fill out any job applications. This can be a DVD, a digital file, or an upload to your personal professional website.

If you want to really sharpen your skills, study the work of the great animation directors past and present, including Walt Disney, Chuck Jones (*Looney Tunes*), and Tim Burton (*The Nightmare Before Christmas*). As you enjoy their work, think about what makes each one's style different from the rest. How do their creations compare to other, less entertaining cartoons? You should also do research to find out how they managed each project, how many members were on their staff, and how each one was received, both critically and commercially.

GETTING PAID

Directors are critical to the success of any animation project, and they'll always be in demand. The animation industry is highly competitive, however, and director jobs are naturally difficult to find. After all, an animated film with a massive budget and dozens of artists still only needs a single director. However, with so much information about the industry now available online, it's easier than ever to get started on your own without a college degree. On top of that, the Bureau of Labor Statistics estimates that opportunities are expected to grow by about 5 percent between 2018 and 2028, which indicates a decent level of optimism for anyone trying to break into the field. The best way to land yourself a director job is to get your foot in the door by working on a smaller production and gradually climbing up the industry ladder.

Because film and TV animations can range in size and scope, the salary of a director is also variable. Experience will also impact overall compensation. In general, you can expect a sizeable paycheck if you're working on a project for a solid company. The average pay for a director in the motion picture

Tim Burton's wild creativity and incredible technical skills have made him one of the most successful animated film directors of all time. Most of his works are instantly recognizable for their unique style and distinct voice.

industry in 2018 was about $84,000. The way this is broken up will be determined in your job contract. You may be paid a set amount weekly during the production process, only be paid after an episode is completed, or given an advance. If you make a name for yourself on many successful projects, you may even receive royalties for your work, getting paid a small amount each time your film or TV show airs.

CHAPTER 10

THE WIDE WORLD OF PRODUCTION

There are many people—and many jobs—involved with any animated production, from a limited-run TV series to a blockbuster feature film. Among the most important of these positions is that of producer. If you're organized and detail oriented, and you'd like to manage a staff of passionate individuals, following this career path may be right for you. As a producer, it'll be your job to help writers, directors, voice-over artists, agents, background artists, and more to collaborate on the same project. On top of that, you'll need to make sure your production stays on schedule and, more importantly, on budget. Studios are quick to pull the plug on anything that takes too long or costs too much. It's the producer's job to make sure the creative vision of the show or film's creator can make it onto the screen efficiently and effectively—all while keeping the artists and staffers happy.

FACTORS OF PRODUCTION

The various responsibilities of a show producer are often rooted in a budget—the amount of money available for a project and a list of how it's expected to be spent. A producer needs to be able to determine the requirements of the production and how to balance the expectations of the writers and actors with the budget. To help understand what a project will need, the producer must work with the show creators to familiarize themselves with the show script and

Most animated projects involve a huge team of artists, writers, managers, and actors. Working on the production side of this industry, you'll be responsible for helping all these individuals work as a team.

concept. From there, the producer hires or approves the selection of key production staff members and will negotiate contracts with voice-over talent and design personnel. Producers must ensure that the production costs don't exceed the budget, and this often means coming up with creative solutions to potentially costly problems.

Since the hired staff on any given project tends to be freelance, a producer must be organized. It's the producer's job to make sure that new employees get added to a company's payroll and that all contracts and other legal documents are in place. Most projects enlist the help of dozens of freelancers, and the producer must manage their workload and schedules. Other responsibilities for the producer may include researching materials that can be used in the show and obtaining legal allowances for use of certain music or sound effects.

GETTING READY

Here are some of the basic skills you should possess and develop if you want to become an animation producer:

- Excellent management and team-building skills
- Excellent verbal and written communication skills
- Excellent creative instincts
- Ability to manage small and large budgets

- Ability to quickly identify and assess problems and find effective solutions
- Ability to negotiate with artists
- Ability to work well under pressure
- Ability to manage multiple assignments while working within deadlines and budgets

Most of these skills can't be taught in school, which is both good and bad news. If you don't think you have these qualities, it'll be hard to find consistent work in this field. If you have what it takes, however, you can make it as a producer without an advanced education. Though many producers have earned a bachelor's degree, on-the-job training is the best education a producer can receive. Here are a few things that you can do if you're interested in following this career path:

- Get an internship at a large company where you can learn about all the tasks

Internships offer young people a lot of advantages, including giving them on-the-job experience and a peek into what the workplace is like.

a producer must oversee and coordinate. Many internships are unpaid, but the hands-on experience you'll gain is well worth the effort. You'll probably even make professional contacts who can help you find paying work.

- Learn as much as you can about the work of a producer in advance. Try to get in contact with experienced producers or people who work at a production company. Do as much reading as you can about the position and its typical responsibilities.
- Accept an entry-level position at a production company, even if it's not directly related to producing. Over time, you may be able to work your way up the ladder.
- Seek out specialized courses in general project management. Though these courses can take time and money, having at least some management education will make you more appealing to studios.
- Start practicing your skills with the various software applications that can help you manage projects as efficiently as possible. Among the basic tools you will want to get acquainted with are Microsoft Word, Microsoft Excel, and budgeting tools that help users plan and track expenses.

GETTING PAID

Show business is centered in several large cities across the United States—mainly Los Angeles and New York—and it's in these locations that the demand for producers is highest. However, there's still work to be found with local or regional television studios, animation studios, film production companies, and independent companies. Other places to explore are Vancouver, Canada, which hosts various animation studios, and Atlanta, Georgia, which is the home of Turner Broadcasting, a major player in TV productions.

Your pay will vary based on the city or region you live in, but an average yearly salary for an animation producer in 2018 was about $84,000. You may receive more or less than this amount depending on the size of your employer and the projects you're assigned to. If you find work in Los Angeles, for example, you'll likely receive a higher salary than someone working for a smaller studio in Ohio.

MANGA

If you're interested in comics, then it's likely you're also familiar with manga. Manga literally means "aimless pictures" in Japanese, but the term refers to a unique comic style that's native to Japan and increasingly popular in the United States and across the globe. It's not to be confused with anime, which is the term for Japanese animated cartoons (though anime does share much of the visual style of manga).

Manga represents the fastest-growing portion of the comic publishing industry, with sales in the United States at well over $100 million each year. In Japan, manga's popularity has elevated its top-selling creators—such as Eiichiro Oda, creator of the popular *One Piece* series—to celebrity status on par with movie stars. Even in a world of increasingly digital book sales, manga volumes have stayed strong. Between 2018 and 2019, for example, Oda's *One Piece* sold more than 12 million copies in Japan.

There are many reasons why manga has captured the attention of so many readers in an international audience. Manga art is often highly stylized and cinematic, with story lines that range from action to fantasy to romance, depending largely on the age and interests of the target audience. It's characterized by a strong line and careful attention to minute details in each panel. Among the most iconic styles of the genre are the large eyes of the characters, a

Eiichiro Oda's *One Piece* series is the best-selling manga of all time, and he's part of the reason why there's such a large global interest in the genre.

trend that began with *Astro Boy* in the 1960s and continues to this day. Some of the titles with a more mature audience, such as Hajime Isayama's *Attack on Titan*, feature nuanced stories and horrifying artwork. Many popular manga have been made into anime movies and TV series, including both *One Piece* and *Attack on Titan*.

Manga comics are commonly printed in black and white and on lower-quality newsprint. In Japanese, they're read from right to left because that's the standard in Japan. Most English translations maintain this right-to-left presentation, which makes it easier for translators and designers to keep the author's original layout.

Manga magazines (or graphic novels) are unique in that they tend to be printed like traditional novels. They're often small, thick volumes that are roughly one-third the dimension of the average American comic book. Most manga are sold in graphic novels that collect five to ten chapters of a series that's been serialized in weekly Japanese manga magazines.

Manga are often created by a single artist, who does everything from imagining the world, writing the story, designing the characters, drawing the manga, and penciling and inking. American comics, by contrast, tend to be produced by an assembly line–like team, are printed in color, and have a more magazine-like appearance with large, glossy pages. The best-selling American comics, such as the classic *Superman* and *Batman*, tend to be superhero works that focus on a single character. Many manga, on the other hand, feature wide casts of unique characters, each of which plays a role in the overall story.

CHAPTER 11

WRITING LETTERS

The process of bringing a beloved Japanese manga to foreign shores is long and complex. There are many people involved, starting with translators. After the words on each manga panel have been translated, the comic must be laid out and the updated words inserted. In addition to filling in speech and thought bubbles, many manga use written sound effects in the background—these must also be translated and reinserted. This kind of work is boring for some, but if you're interested, you may be ready to pursue a career in manga lettering and retouching. As an artist in this field, you'd be contributing to the global spread of manga by making non-Japanese versions look polished and professional.

KEPT IN TRANSLATION

In reading English, we read from left to right. You've probably never given this much thought, but not every country reads text this same way. In Japan,

Akira Toriyama's *Dragon Ball* is one reason why English-language publishers often keep translated manga in the traditional Japanese right-to-left format.

manga is written to be read right to left to better match that country's traditions. Some manga creators, like Akira Toriyama, creator of *Dragon Ball*, have strictly required that their manga be presented to American audiences "unflopped," or in the original right-to-left format. Most manga publishers,

including VIZ and Tokyopop, print their translated manga unflopped. This not only satisfies Japanese authors, it also gives fans a sense of the original version and helps maintain that particular aspect of Japanese culture.

The first step of a letterer's workflow is receiving a translated all-text script. The main part of their job is to take this text and fill in the blank word bubbles of the manga panels with English characters. Modern manga lettering is mainly accomplished by using image editing software on computers. There are a variety of fonts available to you, but the font that a publisher wants to use is typically set well ahead of time. Hand-lettering is still done occasionally, but the task is performed much more quickly, cheaply, and efficiently on a computer with tools like Photoshop and other professional software applications.

Retouching left-to-right formatted work is a more hands-on process and can require the use of physical tools to literally cut and paste pieces of the original artwork and merge them with an English sound effect on the page. Some of the original artwork may need to be totally redrawn by hand. In certain cases, a retouch artist may decide to keep some of the original Japanese sound effects in the American translations. This adds to style and cultural immersion, which may be important for some series.

GETTING READY

If you want to pursue a career in this field, you'll need to have an excellent working knowledge of Japanese entertainment and pop culture (not just manga) before entering the manga industry. If you're considering this position, you probably already have a passion for manga. You'll need to be widely read in the medium, checking out series from all kinds of genres. You may also want to watch as many anime shows and films as you can, as anime and manga are closely connected. The greater your knowledge base, the better job you'll be able to do.

There are countless books, articles, and magazines in bookstores and online that discuss manga's distinctive illustration style. You can learn about the genre's trademark facial features and figures in battle. Even though you won't be writing and illustrating your own original manga, it will be useful for you to understand the basic techniques as you work on retouching existing artwork.

You'll definitely want to have a solid background in figure drawing and some knowledge of lettering fonts and how to create them. Most of all, you should have an excellent eye for detail and the ability to work well with others and within established creative parameters. Letterers and retouch artists don't call the creative shots, but instead faithfully replicate the original creator's vision.

Since the majority of lettering and retouch artists in the United States work as freelancers, you'll have to be self-motivated and have solid communication skills. This will help you consistently find work and become a contributing member of an efficient project team once you've found a position.

Because there's so much technical and artistic work to be done as a letterer, you'd be well served to become proficient in a number of design-related software programs. If you go freelance, your employers will expect you to know a variety of different programs. You'll likely find that advanced computer tools make it easier than ever to start working with manga.

GETTING PAID

Manga has long been a huge success in Japan, and its global popularity has been increasing for years. As more manga series make their way out of Japan and into the hands of American readers, there's going to be increasing demand for lettering and retouch artists to keep pace with industry growth and expansion into new markets. Nevertheless, it will always remain a competitive field in which there are fewer jobs than there are job seekers. To succeed, you'll want to gain as much experience as you can. If you have a solid background in the software publishers use and you can make a strong portfolio of your previous work, potential employers will be more likely to hire you. Whether you're working or in between jobs, you should keep up with the hottest new series and the up-and-coming artists that may come across your desk soon.

If you become a freelance letterer or retouch artist, expect to be paid by the page. Page rates tend to be negotiated with each new employer, and they'll vary according to the publisher or the project. Additionally, you should make sure you're spacing out your workload so you don't have an extremely busy month followed by one with little work. You should also take into account the amount of downtime you may have if the industry slows or jobs become less available to you.

GLOSSARY

anatomy The parts that form a living thing.

cel animation The use of transparent plastic sheets (cels) to draw figures in different states, which creates the illusion of movement when played next to each other.

characterization The way a writer makes a person in a story seem like a real person.

Claymation Animation that features images of clay figures.

cohesive Closely united.

collaborate To work together to achieve a goal.

color palette The selection of colors used for something.

convention A large, organized event that brings together professionals and consumers.

freelance To earn money by being hired to work on different jobs or projects for short periods of time.

genre A category of art or entertainment.

graphic novel Drawings that tell a story and are published in a book.

high resolution Describing digital images of good quality, having a lot of pixels.

line art Art that relies heavily on line segments to create the overall image.

medium The materials or methods used by an artist.

narrative A story.

perspective Point of view.

portfolio A collection of an artist's work that can be shown to employers or fans.

shading The use of dark areas in a drawing.

synchronize To happen at the same time and speed.

3D Short for "three dimensional"; describing figures that have the appearance of depth.

FOR MORE INFORMATION

The Animation Guild
1105 North Hollywood Way
Burbank, CA 91505
(818) 845-7500
Website: https://animationguild.org
Facebook, Instagram, and Twitter:
   @animationguild
This labor union, a branch of the International Alliance of Theatrical Stage Employees, represents artists and animators of all kinds. Its website has more information about workers' rights and workplace regulations for animators.

Comic-Con International
P.O. Box 128458
San Diego, CA 92112
Website: http://www.comic-con.org
Facebook: @comiccon
Instagram and Twitter: @Comic_Con
One of the nation's oldest and largest comic book conventions, San Diego's Comic-Con is one of the industry's top gathering points every year. Its website is a great place to learn more about comics, animation, and manga.

International Animated Film Society (ASIFA–Hollywood)
2114 Burbank Boulevard
Burbank, CA 91506
(818) 842-8330
Website: http://www.asifa-hollywood.org
Facebook, Instagram, and Twitter:
   @ASIFAHollywood

This organization works to encourage people to learn more about animation and spread awareness about the great work done by artists in the field. Its website offers detailed information for aspiring workers and fans of the genre.

Marvel Entertainment
1290 Avenue of the Americas
New York, NY 10104
(212) 576-4000
Website: https://marvel.com
Facebook, Instagram, and Twitter: @Marvel
As one of the oldest and most respected comic book publishers, Marvel's website is an excellent starting point for anyone interested in learning more about the industry.

Screen Actors Guild-American Federation of Television and Radio Artists (SAG-AFTRA)
5757 Wilshire Boulevard, 7th floor
Los Angeles, CA 90036
(855) 724-2387
Website: https://www.sagaftra.org
Facebook, Instagram, and Twitter: @SAGAFTRA
As one of the most prominent labor unions in the United States, SAG-AFTRA was formed to protect the rights and improve the working conditions of writers, actors, and artists of all varieties.

FOR FURTHER READING

Arbona, Alejandro, and Chelsea O'Mara. *Comic Book Creators*. Baltimore, MD: Duo Press, 2019.

Bartolotta, Kenneth. *Anime: Japanese Animation Comes to America*. New York, NY: Lucent Press, 2018.

Burling, Alexis. *Working in Writing*. Mankato, MN: 12 Story Library, 2018.

Campos, Leo. *Creating Manga Comics*. New York, NY: PowerKids Press, 2015.

Gregory, Josh. *Animation: From Concept to Consumer*. New York, NY: Children's Press, 2015.

Horning, Nicole. *A Modern Nerd's Guide to Comic Books*. New York, NY: Gareth Stevens Publishing, 2020.

Kampff, Joseph. *Walt Disney: Legendary Animator and Entertainment Entrepreneur*. New York, NY: Britannica Educational Publishing, 2016.

Kitts, W. L. *Careers in Animation and Comics*. San Diego, CA: ReferencePoint Press, 2020.

Mahaney, Ian F. *Animator*. New York, NY: PowerKids Press, 2015.

INDEX

A

Adobe Photoshop, 30, 32, 36, 37, 62–63, 91
animated films, 4, 5, 6–7, 10, 20, 31, 43, 44, 45, 47–48, 50, 54, 56, 58, 60, 64, 65, 66, 69, 70, 71, 74, 75, 76, 77, 78, 79, 84–85, 86, 87, 92
   Claymation, 42
animator, 5, 51, 58, 60, 73, 74, 75
   becoming a, 61–64
   pay of, 64–65
auditions, 52, 53, 55–56

B

background artist, 5, 66, 75
   becoming a, 67–69
   pay of, 69–70
budget, 42, 76, 79, 64–65, 73, 80, 81, 82, 84

C

casting agency, 52, 56

Claymation, 42, 60, 61, 75
colorist, 5, 12, 30, 31–32, 34, 35, 36
   becoming a, 37–40
   pay of, 40–41
color separation, 35, 36, 38
color theory, 39, 67
competition, 17, 25, 26, 40, 56, 64, 69, 76, 94
convention, comic book, 15, 24, 63
creator, 5, 7, 43, 44, 45–46, 47, 48, 49, 71–72, 75, 79, 80, 86, 90, 93
   becoming a, 47–49
   pay of, 49
Crumb, R. 14, 30–31

D

DC, 6–7, 12, 25
demo, 53, 55, 56, 63
dialogue, 5, 9, 10, 46, 60
director, 5, 52, 63, 67, 71, 75, 79
   becoming a, 74–76
   duties of, 71–74

pay of, 76–78
Disney, Walt, 75, 76

E
education, 4, 27, 47, 54, 61, 82, 84

F
figure drawing classes, 24, 61, 93
freelancer, 18, 24, 26, 33, 64–65, 81, 93, 94

G
graphic novels, 6, 12, 14, 88

I
inkers, 5, 12, 23, 27–29, 30–31, 34
  becoming a, 31–32
  pay of, 33

J
Japan, manga in, 4, 5, 86, 87–88, 89–91, 92, 93–94

L
layout, 20, 22, 25, 27, 67–68, 72, 88
letterers, 5, 93, 94
  workflow of, 91
line art, 25, 38
Looney Tunes, 47, 76

M
Marvel, 6–7, 10, 14, 25, 26, 40
films, 17
Mickey Mouse, 44, 50, 75
mood, 6, 20, 34, 39, 40, 67

N
narrative, 9, 10–11
newspapers, comic strips, 6, 8

O
One Piece, 86, 87

P
pencillers, 5, 10, 12, 19–20, 23, 27–29, 31, 32, 33, 34

becoming a, 23–25
pay of, 25–26
perspective, 20, 24, 67, 68
plot, 5, 6, 9, 10, 23, 45
popularity
　of animated entertainment, 4, 49
　of comics, 6, 8, 12, 14, 40, 41
　of manga, 5, 86, 87, 93
　tools, 32, 37, 59–60
portfolio, 24, 69, 76, 94
practice, 8, 15, 27, 32, 33, 53, 61, 69, 75–76, 84
producers, 5, 46, 49, 52, 73, 75, 79, 80–81
　becoming a, 81–84
　pay of, 84–85
publishers, 6–7, 8, 12, 15, 17, 18, 24–25, 26, 33, 40, 41, 94
　independent, 12, 25
　manga, 90–91

S

Sandman, 12
Screen Actors Guild-American Federation of Television and Radio Artists (SAG-AFTRA), 57
script, 10, 12, 15–16, 19, 20, 23, 34, 45–47, 48, 52, 56, 71, 80–81, 91
scriptwriters, 5, 9, 10, 12, 20, 25, 27–28, 34
　becoming a, 14–16
　pay of, 17–18
shading techniques, 31, 38, 64, 67
show bible, 45
software, 15–16, 30, 32, 33, 35, 36, 37, 38, 40, 42, 48, 53, 59–60, 62, 67, 68, 73, 84, 91, 93, 94
sound effects, 51, 55, 60, 72, 74, 81, 89, 91–92
Spider-Man, 6
Spider-Man, 14
SpongeBob Squarepants, 42, 47
storyboard, 46, 47, 52, 70, 71, 72, 74
streaming services, 12, 49
studio

animation, 45, 48–49, 52, 53, 79, 84
production, 56, 57
recording, 55
television, 84–85
submission guidelines, 15, 24
superheroes, 6, 84
Superman, 6, 22
Superman, 22, 25, 88

T
talent agency, 52, 53, 55, 56
3D animation, 5, 60, 67, 75
Toy Story, 42, 60
training, 8, 37, 53, 60, 69, 82
translation, 10, 19–20, 25, 88, 89–92
tutorials, 37, 38–39, 48
TV shows, 4, 5, 10, 43, 49, 50, 58, 66, 70, 74, 78
two-dimensional animation, 5, 58, 59–60, 67, 75

U
United States
comics in, 4, 93
entertainment industry in, 57, 84
manga in, 86

V
vision, 8, 19, 27–28, 31, 71, 74, 79, 93
voice-over actor, 5, 43, 47, 50, 54, 75, 79, 81
becoming a, 52–53, 55–56
pay of, 56–57
process for, 51–52
voice tracks, 51–52

W
Walt Disney Studios, 54, 75

Y
Yellow Kid, The, 8

ABOUT THE AUTHOR

Siyavush Saidian lives with his wife and two corgis in New York. A lover of books and writing, he knew college was the right path for him, but he realizes that's not the case for everyone. He's excited to help young people find jobs they love, just like he did.

CREDITS

Cover (icon background) LuckyVector/Shutterstock.com; cover (main image) portishead1/Getty Images; p. 7 nikkimeel/Shutterstock.com; p. 11 Fabio Principe/Shutterstock.com; p. 13 Kevin Nixon/SFX Magazine/Future via Getty Images; p. 16 Sam Aronov/Shutterstock.com; p. 21 harpazo_hope/Getty Images; p. 22 Hulton Archive/Handout/Getty Images; p. 29 BublikHaus/Shutterstock.com; p. 30 Eamonn McCabe/Popperfoto/Getty Images; p. 36 Alex Ste/Shutterstock.com; p. 39 Monstar Studio/Shutterstock.com; p. 43 Gorodenkoff/Shutterstock.com; p. 46 Rene Johnston/Toronto Star/Getty Images; p. 51 David Fuentes Prieto/Shutterstock.com; p. 54 PhotoQuest/Getty Images; p. 59 FrameStockFootages/Shutterstock.com; p. 62 andresr/Getty Images; p. 68 George Dolgikh/Shutterstock.com; p. 72 weedezign/Shutterstock.com; p. 77 Barry King/WireImage/Getty Images; p. 80 Rawpixel.com/Shutterstock.com; p. 83 Gorodenkoff/Shutterstock.com; p. 87 Awana JF/Shutterstock.com; p. 90 Pabkov/Shutterstock.com

Designer: Brian Garvey; Editor: Siyavush Saidian